It started with a P

by
Brittany Pomales
illustrated by
Andrew Joyner

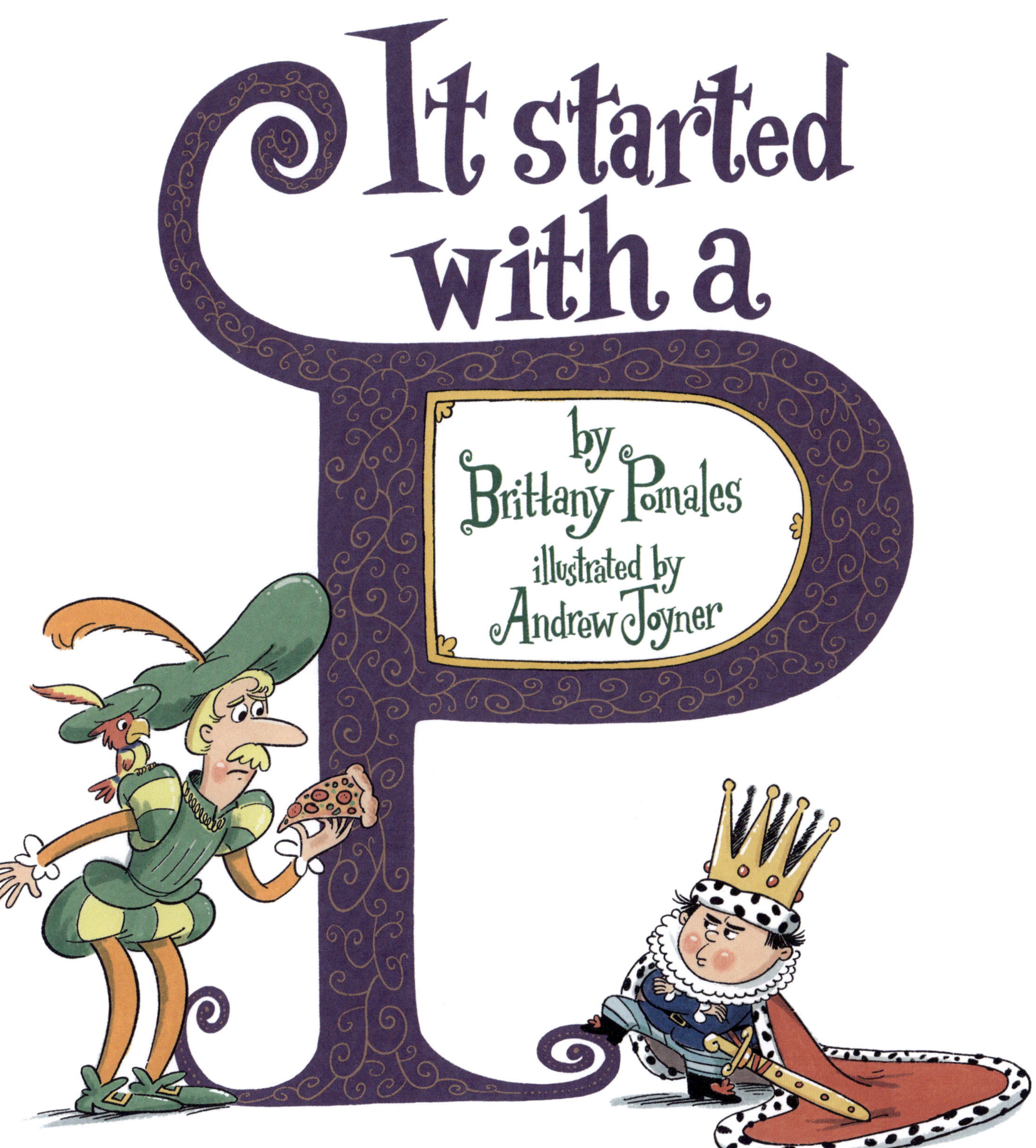

SCHOLASTIC

To my father, Greg, who shaped my sense of humour,
and to Lavalle for filling my heart with laughter —B. P.

For Beck, Will, and Charlotte —A. J.

Scholastic Australia
PO Box 579 Gosford NSW 2250
ABN 11 000 614 577
www.scholastic.com.au

Part of the Scholastic Group
Sydney · Auckland · New York · Toronto · London · Mexico City
· New Delhi · Hong Kong · Buenos Aires · Puerto Rico

Published by Scholastic Australia in 2025.

Published by arrangement with Flamingo Books, an imprint of Penguin Young Readers Group, a division of Penguin Random House LLC.

ISBN 978-1-76164-456-6

Printed in China by Dream Colour Printing.

Scholastic Australia's policy, in association with Dream Colour, is to use papers that are renewable and made efficiently with wood from responsibly managed sources, so as to minimise its environmental footprint.

10 9 8 7 6 5 4 3 2 1 25 26 27 28 29 / 2

It started with a P

The night before his birthday, King Liam had a **peculiar** dream. He **pondered** its meaning over **pancakes**.

"I had a terrible nightmare! I dreamed my birthday was ruined!"

"What ruined it, Your Majesty?" asked Cedric, King Liam's royal advisor.

"Well, I don't remember. BUT it started with the letter **P**."

"**Perhaps** a **pigeon**? A **popcorn** kernel? A **piranha**?"

"I don't know!" the king said with a sigh.

So he made a drastic decision.

"Everything that starts with the letter **P** must go."

Cedric had **plenty** of experience with King Liam's king-size meltdowns. Who could forget the frozen treat fiasco?

And then there was the kingdom-wide balloon ban.

But of all King Liam's overreactions, this celebration crisis took the cake.

So it was no surprise that Cedric was not **particularly pleased** about this **predicament**.

"Everything? Even the **pepperoni pizzas** for tonight's **party**?"
"**Party!**" exclaimed King Liam. "How could we **possibly** have a **party** at a time like this?"

And so Cedric began to **purge** the **palace** of Ps.

He tossed the **pepperoni pizzas** out the window.

He donated all the king's **presents**.

When he got to the **piñata**,
Cedric couldn't resist.

THWACK.

"Oh no! **Popping** candy!"

Cedric shooed the **pigeons perched** on the **parapet** and fished the **piranhas** from the moat.

He gathered all the **pants** in the kingdom.

Long **pants**,

short **pants**,

old **pants**,

new **pants**,

scaredy **pants**,

smarty **pants**,

fancy **pants**,

and last but not least,

his own **pants**.

And fed them to the royal goat,

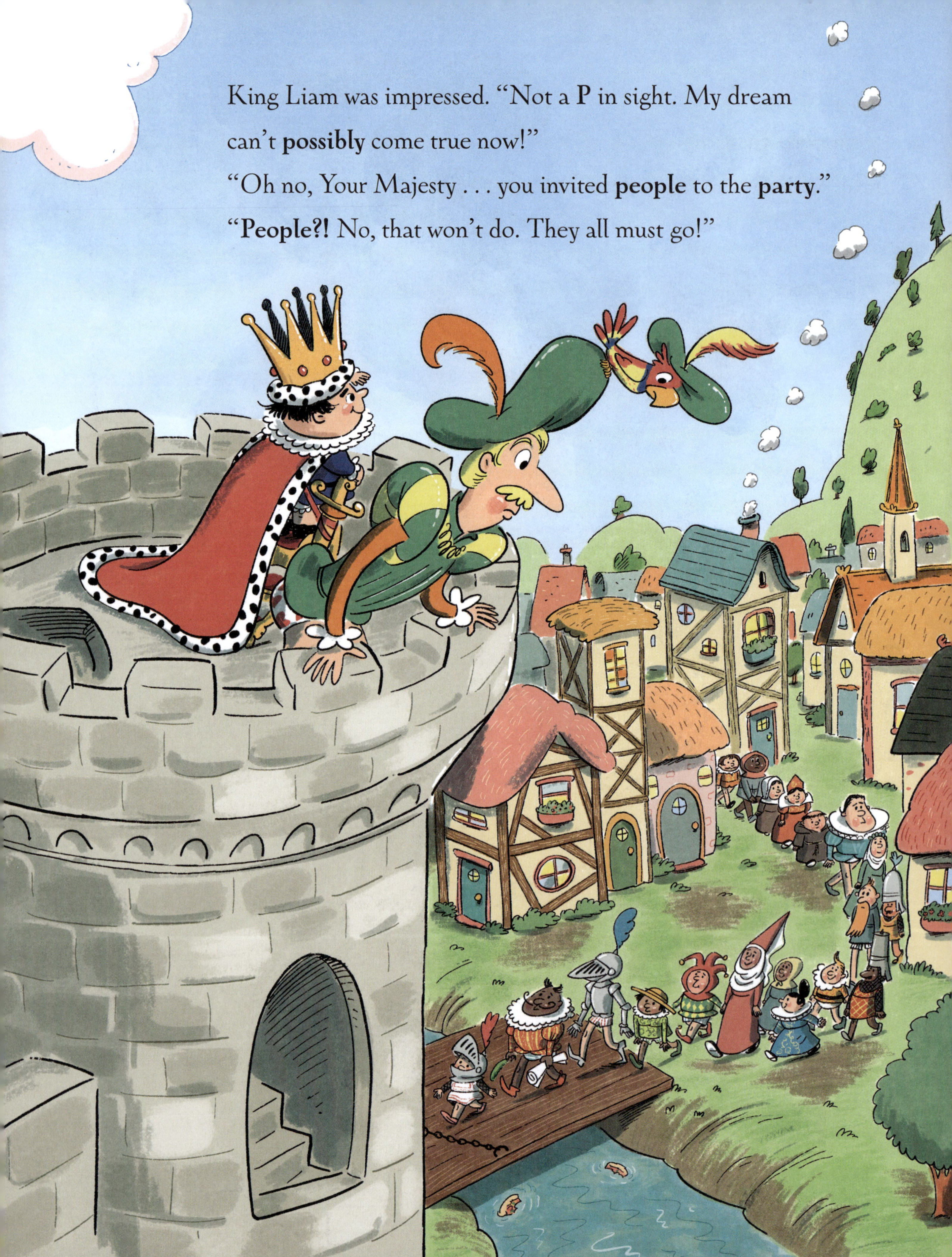

King Liam was impressed. “Not a **P** in sight. My dream can’t **possibly** come true now!”

“Oh no, Your Majesty . . . you invited **people** to the **party**.”

“**People?!** No, that won’t do. They all must go!”

"I suppose, then,
Your Majesty, this is goodbye."
"Don't be silly, Cedric.
You're my royal advisor.
Advisor starts with an A."

And so Cedric guided the kingdom's entire **population** to the **pier**.

The **people protested**.

The **poets protested** in rhyme.

They were **puzzled**, **peeved**, and **pushing** back.

"This is **preposterous**."

Then a small **peep** rose from the crowd: "Even me?"

The king **paused** for a moment.

"I'm sorry, sis. But you're a **princess**."

Cedric **packed** the **princess**, the **people**, and their **pets** into **paddle boats**.

Including his own **pet parrot**.

“Farewell, **Polly**!”

Ridding the **palace** of Ps had been a lot of work. Cedric collapsed into his chair beside the throne. "All the Ps have been removed from the **palace**, Your Majesty."

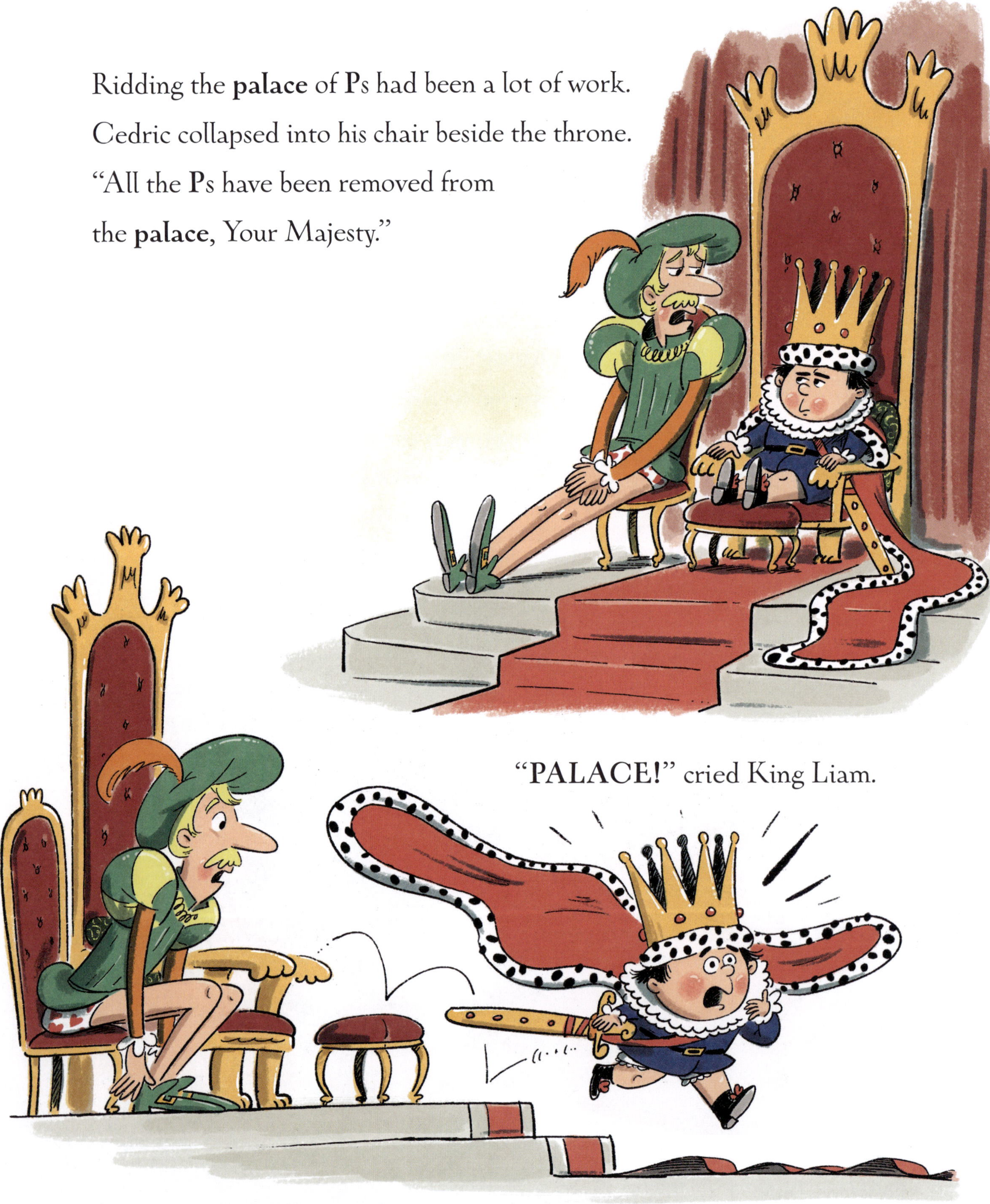

"**PALACE!**" cried King Liam.

So His Majesty **packed** his things—everything that didn't start with a **P**, of course—and departed for a desert island.

There he sat. Not a **P** in sight.

No **pals**.

No **presents**.

No **party**.

King Liam was all alone . . .

On his birthday.

That's when it came to him.

"Aha! I remembered my dream!

I know what the **P** is!"

The king **packed** his things and sailed back to the **palace**.

Along the way, he reunited with the **princess**, gathered the **people** and their **pets**, and **plunged** the **piranhas** back into the moat.

Then King Liam burst into the **palace**.

"Your Majesty, welcome back!"

"Cedric, I have remembered my dream."

The **people** listened in anticipation.

“The **problematic P** is . . .

"**PARTY POOPER!!!**"

"A **party pooper?**" asked Cedric.

"**Precisely!** I was so worried that something would ruin the **party** that I became the very **problem** I tried so hard to **prevent.** I was the **party pooper** all along."

“But now you’re not,” **proclaimed** the **princess**.
“Just in time for cake. Make a wish, Liam!”

King Liam **puffed** and **puffed**.

But one little candle did not blow out.

So King Liam did what he always did when things didn't go his way.

"CEDRIC! Every candle in the castle—

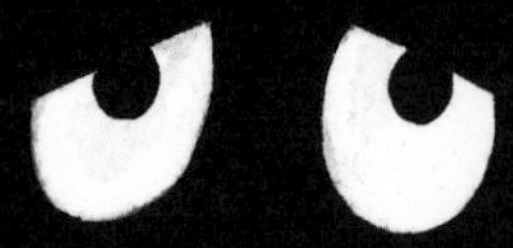

must go.